WISE WORDS OF
PAUL TIULANA

- An Inupiat Alaskan's Life -

WISE WORDS OF
PAUL TIULANA
~ An Inupiat Alaskan's Life ~

BY VIVIAN SENUNGETUK

IN THEIR OWN OWN VOICES

FRANKLIN WATTS • A Division of Grolier Publishing

New York   London   Hong Kong   Sydney   Danbury, Connecticut

Frontis: Paul Tiulana at age seventeen

Royalities derived from this book will be divided equally between Vivian Senungetuk and the family of Paul Tiulana.

Photographs ©: Anchorage Daily News: 7, 68, 73; Pontificia Fotografia: 9; Santa Clara Univer Archives/The Hubbard Collection: cover, 2, 11, 12, 13, 15, 16, 17, 18, 19, 20, 21, 23, 24, 25, 26, 30, 31, 32, 34, 36 top, 36 bottom, 40, 41, 43, 44, 47, 48, 50, 53, 55, 56, 59, 61, 64, 65, 70.

Map by: XNR Productions, Inc.

Library of Congress Cataloging-in-Publication Data
Senungetuk, Vivian.
    Wise words of Paul Tiulana : an Inupiat Alaskan's life / by Vivian Senungetuk ; photographs b Bernard R. Hubbard.
        p.   cm.
    "An earlier version of this book was published as A place for winter ... by the CIRI Foundatio 1987" — T.p. verso.
    Includes bibliographical references and index.
    Summary: Presents the life of an Alaskan hunter, storyteller, craftsman, and traditional leader who grew up on King Island, Alaska, in the 1920s.
    ISBN 0-531-11448-1
    1. Tiulana, Paul, 1921-   —Juvenile literature. 2. Inuit—Alaska—Ukivok—Biography—Juv nile literature. 3. Inuit—Alaska—Ukivok—Juvenile literature. 4. Ukivok (Alaska)—Social life a customs. [1. Tiulana, Paul, 1921- . 2. Inuit—Alaska—Ukivok. 3. Eskimos—Alaska—Ukivok. Ukivok (Alaska)—Social life and customs.] I. Tiulana, Paul, 1921- . II. Hubbard, Bernard Rose crans, 1888-1962, ill. III. Tiulana, Paul, 1921-   Place for winter. IV. Title.
E99.E7T528 1998
979.8'6—DC21   97-51

An earlier version of this book was published as
A Place for Winter: Paul Tiulana's Story
by The CIRI Foundation in 1987.

Published simultaneously in Canada

Printed in the United States of America

1 2 3 4 5 6 7 8 9 10 R 07 06 05 04 03 02 01 00 99 98

CONTENTS

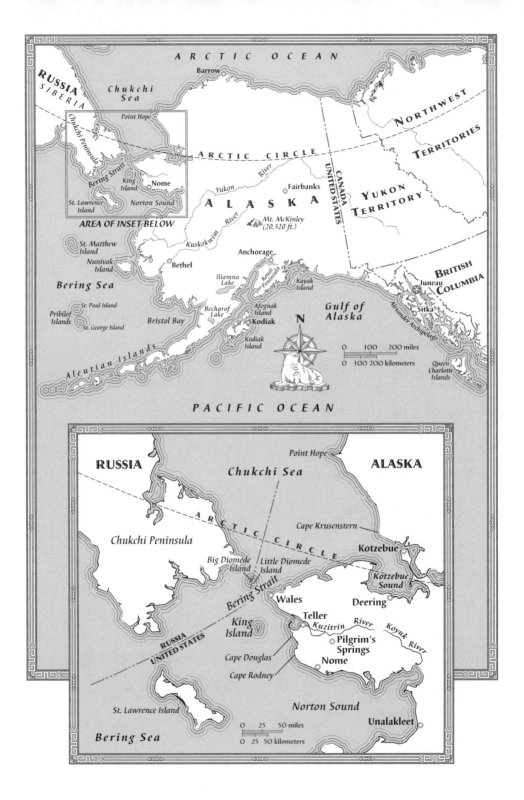

ARCTIC OCEAN

RUSSIA
SIBERIA

Chukchi
Sea

Barrow

NORTHWEST

TERRITORIES

Point Hope

Chukchi Peninsula

ARCTIC CIRCLE

CANADA
UNITED STATES

YUKON

TERRITORY

Bering Strait

King
Island

Nome

Yukon

River

Fairbanks

ALASKA

St. Lawrence
Island

Norton Sound

AREA OF INSET BELOW

Kuskokwim

Mt. McKinley
(20,320 ft.)

River

BRITISH
COLUMBIA

St. Matthew
Island

Nunivak
Island

Bethel

Anchorage

Kenai
Peninsula

Kayak
Island

Juneau

Bering Sea

Iliamna
Lake

Alexander Archipelago

Sitka

Pribilof
Islands

St. Paul Island

St. George Island

Bristol Bay

Becharof
Lake

Afognak
Island

Kodiak

Gulf of
Alaska

N

Kodiak
Island

Aleutian Islands

0   100   200 miles

0 100 200 kilometers

Queen
Charlotte
Islands

PACIFIC OCEAN

RUSSIA

Point Hope

Chukchi Sea

ALASKA

ARCTIC CIRCLE

Chukchi Peninsula

Cape Krusenstern

Kotzebue

Big Diomede
Island

Little Diomede
Island

Kotzebue
Sound

Bering Strait

Wales

Deering

King
Island

Teller

Kuzitrin   River

Koyuk
River

RUSSIA
UNITED STATES

Cape Douglas

Pilgrim's
Springs

Nome

Cape Rodney

St. Lawrence Island

Norton Sound

Unalakleet

Bering Sea

0   25   50 miles

0   25   50 kilometers

PAUL TIULANA'S STORY

This is the story of a Native American hero named Paul Tiulana. Paul was born in 1921 on an island in the Bering Sea off the coast of Alaska. The island was named Ooq-vok, meaning "a place for winter," in the language of his people, the Inupiat. It was later named King Island by the white people, and Paul's people were called Eskimos. It is hard to know how long his people had lived on King Island. Maybe they had lived there for hundreds of years; maybe they had lived there for thousands of years.

Paul told his story when he was sixty-five years old. He was a gifted man in many ways. He understood his culture, his people, his family, his religion, and his country. He served all of these throughout his life. Paul spoke English well, even

Paul and Clara Tiulana in 1959

though he finished only a few years of school. The words in this book are his, edited only slightly. As Paul's biographer, I, along with his daughter, Lillian Tiulana, and his sister-in-law, Helen Pushruk, have added some explanations and background information in brackets.

When speaking English, Paul referred to himself as Eskimo or as Native. For many years, the term Inuit has been used to identify northern people in Canada, and the term Inupiat is used in Alaska. Paul did not care which terms were used. He knew who he was and what he was talking about. He was informed and polite, and people listened to him wherever he went.

In this book Paul tells about his early life on King Island. He tells how he was taught as a child to behave, to take care of himself on the mountain of King Island and on the ice surrounding it, to hunt, to respect the traditions of his people, and to live as Eskimo people had lived since the beginning of time. He recalls the coming of the first white person to the island—a priest—and the effects of World War II on his people.

Paul moved with his family to Anchorage when he was forty-six years old. He worked in the city as a counselor and a teacher of Native culture. He was a well-known carver and leader of the King Island Dancers, a folk-dance group that performed at museums and cultural events all over the United States. He spent much of his time teaching children and adults what he had learned while growing up on King Island.

Paul did not take much part in politics. He was an old-fashioned leader who worked directly with the people. Remembering the past, he compared it with the present, analyzed changes, and worked for a better future for what he called "our Native people."

When Pope John Paul II visited Alaska in 1981, he was greeted by Inupiat and Yupik women who gave him a **parka**. Clara Tiulana (far left) did most of the sewing. The parka cover was made of white camouflage cotton. The lining was white rabbit fur. The trim around the hood was wolverine fur.

In the later years of his life, Paul was honored by two presidents of the United States, the government of England, the Alaska Federation of Natives, the Alaska State Legislature, and the Catholic Archbishop of Anchorage. And Paul's wife, Clara, was introduced to Pope John Paul II when he visited Anchorage.

The Roman Catholic Church played an important part in the history of King Island. As Paul explains, the priests who came to King Island appreciated and encouraged the people there. They incorporated Native culture into church practices.

The wonderful historical photographs in this book were taken by a Jesuit priest, Father Bernard Hubbard, who lived on King Island between 1937 and 1939. A sketch of his life appears on page 73.

A sketch of his life appears on page 73.

⮜Vivian Senungetuk

~1~

A Place for Winter

My name is Paul Tiulana. I am from King Island. King Island is in the Bering Sea, northwest of Nome, Alaska. We Eskimos have lived there as long as anybody can remember. Our Eskimo name for King Island is Ooq-vok, which means "a place for winter." It is a rocky place and steep. We built our houses on stilts because there was no flat area anywhere on the island.

I was born sixty-five years ago [in 1921], before any white people lived on King Island. They named me Tiulana, after my grandfather. This is my Eskimo name. When I was baptized, the priest gave me the name Paul. That is my Christian name, and everybody calls me Paul now.

I can remember back to when I was seven or eight years old. I remember what the older folks said to me. In living I was taught to be respectful to others. I was taught to follow all the rules about living in the village so that I would be a respected person in the future. You see, if I did not obey the rules and help the older folks, they would be inclined not to help me. The more I obeyed their counseling, the more they gave me their ideas as I grew up. Every day counseling came from my uncles and aunts and grandfathers. My cousins had to counsel me also.

If we obeyed the older persons, they made us toys. When they saw that we were going to be really obedient persons, they gave us what we wanted, even if it was something hard to make. My father made a bow and arrow for me. In the springtime, about April, when the **snowbirds**

This is King Island. It is in the Bering Sea, thirty-five miles from the Alaskan mainland. The island is two and a half miles long. The only village faces south. It is the best place in the world to lose weight and get away from city life.

This is the village. The big building is the church. The larger houses were built by Father Hubbard for his staff. On the lower left is the schoolhouse. At the right, the doorway dug into the hill led to a clubhouse where we did ivory carving, made hunting equipment, and dried sealskins in winter.

To climb from the upper houses down to the sea takes five minutes when you are young and ten to fifteen minutes when you are old.

came to King Island, we would hunt them with bows and arrows. And
every time we killed a little bird, we made a notch in the bow so we could
tell how many birds we killed year to year. My mother cooked the birds
for us. I was obedient for the older persons, and they made me the really
good arrows that I wanted.

I lost my father when I was nine. He went out hunting on the ice and
never came back. From then on my uncle Olanna, my father's brother, called
me "Dad." Everybody called me Dad even though I was a little boy.

I had a few relatives who counseled me when they visited my mother so that everything would be good for me in the future. Uncle Panatok, one of the respected persons to me, was second cousin to my father. He would come to our house and ask me, "Did your mother spank you this morning or say some hard words to you?"

Even if my mother had not spanked me, I would say that she had. Then my uncle would go to my mother and say, "Do not scold your son!" You see, the way my uncle and my mother were related, on the family tree, they were supposed to tease each other. They were what we called **cross-cousins**. That made my uncle my right-hand man. He told my mother not to scold me. "When you hurt Dad's feelings, you hurt my feelings," he would say to her. So even though my mother had not spanked me, my uncle's teasing of her gave me a little comfort.

My mother, Annie Kattac, is picking some flowers. She cooked these sour-tasting greens in water and put them in barrels. In the wintertime she took them out and mixed them with seal oil and reindeer fat.

~2~
NAMING THE MONTHS

At King Island we lived by the weather. We had certain activities every month, and we named the months according to the activities and the weather.

I will start with October. The name for October in the King Island dialect of the Eskimo language means "icy month." We call it icy month because ice starts to form among the rocks below the village at this time. The ice starts forming at the bottom of the Bering Sea. [The ice then floats up to the surface. As winter deepens, the surface freezes over.]

We call November "going up to the back of the island to hunt there." November is the month when the wind starts blowing really hard from the north, blowing ice up against the island on the north side and away from the island on the south side. The ice around the south side can move, so it is not safe to try to walk there. The ones who have walked there have drifted out on the young ice and never come back. They drowned out in the water when the wind started blowing hard from the north and waves crushed the ice out in the Bering Sea.

In the fall of the year we did not walk too far out on the ice in any direction unless we carried kayaks with us. November was "going up to the back of the island to hunt there" because it was safer to hunt on the back, or north, side of King Island then. We worked on our furs in the fall, so that we could have new mukluks, or boots, new seal pants, and

Susrak is cutting a female walrus hide for boats, using a woman's knife called an **ulu**. Her mukluks are fancy—made of sealskin with bleached sealskin trim.

My uncle, John Olanna, is performing the Half Mask Dance. In the background there are nine singers and drummers. The dance was kind of comical to make people laugh.

LEFT PAGE 🖝 Leo Kunnuk, Jr. performs during a polar bear dance. Any child or adult could join the dancing.

new parkas, or coats. We renewed some of the hunting equipment to use in the winter.

December we call "dancing month." We started to dance in December because everything on King Island was ready for winter. Our houses were ready. We had put our **skin boats** up in racks. We had stored our things for the winter. We danced in the month of December and through the winter to some old songs and some new ones. We prepared new songs for the show we put on for other Eskimo people on the mainland in the summer.

These boys are lining up to slide down the hill on the polar-bear skin. This was in December or January, when we had only about six hours of daylight every day.

Our houses were built of wood. The living quarters were about ten feet by ten feet. The roof and the back of the house were covered with walrus hide to insulate the house from the wind. In front of the house sealskins and a polar-bear hide are being weather-dried and bleached.

January we call "reverse dance month." The people on King Island say that long ago they tapped the drums with the opposite hand in January. I do not know why they did it. I have never seen it, but I have been told that it was done that way.

The older men hunted seal and polar bear in January. When a hunter got a polar bear, an old person would tell a story while the women cleaned the skin. We cooked and ate the meat and saved the skin. We cut a hole in the ice and pushed the skin down into it. The little shrimps in the water ate the blood and excess fat from the skin. We would leave the skin down in the water for a couple of days. Then we pulled it out, cleaned it off with snow, and squeezed the salt water from the hair. After we did this, we took the skin up the hill and slid down on it. About a dozen children rode on that bear skin; we slid down over and over until just before sundown. Then the hunter who got the polar bear came and rolled up the skin and stored it underneath his skin boat until March.

The older persons also hunted seals in January. When they got a one-year-old seal, they would use the skin for sealskin pants. The fur is a bit longer on a young seal and so the pants last longer. The skin of a female seal was used for mukluks and mittens because it is lighter. When they killed an older male seal, they worked to bleach the skin and then used it to make parkas. They put the skin in the water for about three days, then they rinsed off the excess fat and pulled it out. Next they put the skin outside on a rack in front of the house and left it to freeze during the night. Bleached skins were left outside in the winter to cure and dry.

The month of February is "the month of the prematurely born seal"—that means the seal pup is born too early. Sometimes seals miscarry in February. In this month the older men mostly went seal hunting. The seal-

Bernard Kasignoc is preparing his kayak for spring hunting. He is working on top of his house. Bernard was both a cross-cousin and a partner-cousin to me. Mostly he was a cross-cousin to me at King Island; that is, he used to tease me. But when someone from the mainland came, who was a cross-cousin to both of us, Bernard became my partner-cousin and we worked together.

skin is prime during the months of January and February.

The month of March we call "fixing our kayaks for springtime." During this month we repaired everything on our kayaks. We renewed our **harpoons** and our harpoon lines. If we did not want to change the skin on our kayaks, we applied **blubber** over the skins. We could do this only a couple of times because a third time could burn the skin. If we put too much oil on the skin, it started to get soft and easy to tear. We tried to get everything ready for the spring hunt.

These hunting kayaks were left on the shore ice after the hunters came in because they would be used again the next morning. The lances with hooks were used to pull the kayaks up against the edge of the ice. They were also used to test young ice.

April is "the month for going out hunting with our kayaks." When the seals are born in the first part of April, the ice stops forming around the island. It does not freeze anymore. When that happened we went out with our kayaks, hunting mostly for oogruks, or big bearded seals.

Toward the end of April we began to see some walruses on top of the ice, coming from the south. It was an exciting time. The men hardly slept—only about two or three hours at night before they woke up to go hunting. The days started to get longer in April as the sun rose earlier in the morning and set later at night.

Even in the month of April we still danced once in a while because we did not have much to do. If the weather was bad, sometimes we danced for the weather to calm down. We tried to do something by dancing, to pass time. Sometimes when we danced to make the weather good, we timed it right and the weather was good the next day. Even in my days, we danced outdoors for the weather to be good.

One time we had weather from the north blowing for a couple of weeks—bad weather. The men were kind of curious, kind of disappointed. One night they said they were going to dance for the weather, maybe something like praying. They danced all night, and in about three days the weather was good.

The month of May we call "the ice starts to melt from the island." The first part of May we still tried to hunt for oogruks, the big bearded seals, with our kayaks. It is easier to get the seals with kayaks, not walking. We brought in more meat in May, putting the seals in our kayaks and, when we reached land, dragging them with our sleds.

Toward the end of May we started going out for walrus. We also rebuilt our skin boats. We made new frames and covered the boats with new skins. We had two kinds of boats at King Island—kayaks and skin boats. The kayaks were lightweight one-person canoes. Skin boats were large, maybe thirty feet long and six feet wide, and heavy. They were made of

Ignatius Annayuk is
eating a **murre** egg.
We collected the eggs in
June. The murres laid them
in little nooks and
on rock ridges on the cliffs.

These men are building a new skin boat in the month of May. The frame is made of driftwood tied together with rawhide. The man on the right is Charles Tigmeak.

driftwood frames covered by split walrus hides. After the ice began to break up, we started to use the skin boats. They were safer than kayaks in open water, out hunting. Sometimes a sudden storm came up and we had a long way to paddle. We could manage in kayaks, but we preferred to hunt with the skin boat when the ice was scattering. Also, we could bring in more meat with the skin boat. At this time we hardly slept.

A long time ago, when the women worked on the meat that the hunters brought in, they slept on the rocks at night because they did not have

Twenty-two King Islanders are going to Nome on Nereruk's boat. The trip took thirteen hours with an outboard motor. The sails are ready in case the winds are right. An empty **seal poke** hangs over the side.

time to walk back to their houses. They would have wasted time going back and forth. They cut the meat on the rocks and slept there, too. The older girls stayed home to take care of the young children. Only after they finished their cutting did the women go back to their homes.

We call the month of June "unnoticed moon." In June everything was so busy we did not have time to think what day it was. We worked on preparing our walrus meat—putting it into caves for preservation—so that we would have more meat for the next year. We worked so hard that

we did not notice the month. We hardly thought about anything but working on the walrus meat and skins.

July is "the month of going over to the mainland." We went over to the mainland in our skin boats to see our friends there, to trade with them, and to dance. We practiced new dances in the winter to show them in the summer. We had a sort of contest to see who could make up the best dance.

Before we left for the mainland, we picked the wild greens and preserved them for winter use. We put our plants in seal oil; they were preserved in that oil and did not spoil. We made Eskimo ice cream with one plant. It was done like this: We made a container out of walrus hide. Then, while the plant was still frozen, we pounded it with a walrus tusk. Then we mixed it with reindeer fat and seal oil. We used it when we were eating seal or oogruk. Delicious!

We do not have a name for the month of August. We were still visiting on the mainland then. We could pick berries there—blackberries, blueberries, salmonberries. I call August "berry-picking month."

September we call "ready to go back to the island." We planned to go back to the island in the early fall, while the weather was good, because by October, the Bering Sea gets really rough. Also, we tried to go back to the island in the month of September so that we would have time to winterize our houses.

Mary Ann Pushruk and Agatha Patunac are picking salmonberries on the top of the island.

THE ICE NEVER SLEEPS

When I was about ten years old, my uncles and my older brother began to teach me how to survive out on the ice when I was hunting. They taught me what I had to do when I went out hunting by myself, what I needed to do with my clothes, and what the weather would do to me if I drifted out from King Island on the ice. You see, the ice forms on the Bering Sea around the island, but the ocean underneath is always moving. They taught me the survival techniques that I would have to use if I drifted out on the **moving ice**. They said, "The ice never sleeps; the current never sleeps."

Sometimes my uncle Olanna trained me. He walked with me all day long without stopping. He wanted me to build my body to run long distances without stopping. I had to hold my breath for long distances while walking. That is one of the survival techniques we worked on. I was not supposed to smoke because smoking is bad for your breath. You get exhausted in maybe fifteen minutes if you smoke when you are young. Holding your breath while walking builds your lungs for long-distance running.

If we were hunting south of the island and the north wind started to blow, we had to start running back to the island. The wind from the north pushes the ice away from the south of the island and the sea opens up. If we ran out of breath and had to stop in five minutes, there might be an open **lead**, open water, between us and the island. We would not be able to

The King Island boys' football team

Frances is my half-sister. She is pointing at a king crab. We used to tie bait—young bullheads [fish] cut in half—on a line made of **baleen** from the mouth of a whale. We put a sinker on the line and dropped it. When the crab grabbed it, we pulled up the line. Later Frances married an outside person from the lower forty-eight states.

cross it. We had to run constantly, maybe five miles, maybe ten miles, without stopping at all, carrying our hunting bags, until we reached a safe point. Everything about us had to be prepared for our survival.

My uncle Olanna took me out when I was eleven years old and taught me how the currents move around the island. He taught me to know the directions of the wind. In front of King Island there is shore ice and some rocks and big boulders that stick out from the shore ice. He told me to mark the rocks, to line up objects with my eyes. Then if we drifted too far, we could look for the markers on the rocks and we would know which way to walk to be in a safe place.

One day my uncle Olanna took me out on the ice for two or three hours to hunt seals. I was a really bad shot with a rifle. I missed every time a seal came up. My uncle was frustrated with me and took me back to the village. Then he went out again to get some seals himself. That is the way I was taught when I was young.

Thin new ice will form on top of the leads, or open water.

*J*ohn Olanna, my uncle, holds paddles and harpoon lines for his skin boat. He had a skin disease and his face turned white. Then he burned in the sun.

Sometimes he wore a cotton scarf over his nose and mouth for protection. He was a good hunter and a good teacher for me. He became the first president of the King Island Council, which was formed in 1934.

The women taught me some hunting techniques, too—things that had been told to them by their fathers when they were small. They explained to me what their fathers had told them about hunting survival. I never read those things; they were not written down. I had to memorize them.

I was taught another thing by my mother. She said, "Son, there are two barrels out in the shed that were kept filled by your father, filled full of blubber." She encouraged me to be like my father. My father was one of the great hunters on King Island and I wanted to be like him. I tried every way to be like my father. Even though I was sometimes really tired, with tears in my eyes, I tried to keep up with the others out hunting.

I was taught not to take a nap during the day because then, in the future, when I grew up, I would be infected with sleepiness during the day. If I went out hunting and stayed out for a couple of days, then rode in my kayak, I might get sleepy and tip over. So whenever I lay down, my uncle Akilena called me and said, "Dad, get up! You'd better not take a nap. It is not good for you." And even though I was really sleepy, I would try to get up and do something.

Edward Mukoyuk sleeping in the sunlight.

The next step, when I was about sixteen, was to learn how to ride in a kayak, a one-person canoe. My uncle taught me. We practiced how to ride it in the springtime when the ice was gone from the island and the weather was good, calm. Sometimes I asked my uncle if I could ride a kayak. He said, "Go ahead, as long as somebody goes with you. If you tip over and there is nobody around, you will drown."

Going out hunting in a kayak is something else. In the spring, when the people of the village spotted walrus, the men started out fast. A dead walrus is very heavy to pull behind a kayak, so the hunters tried to reach the animals when they were as close to the island as possible, right in sight of the island. When the men started to go out to hunt walrus, the older hunters never stopped. They paddled hard, following the herd of walrus. If they went out too far from the island, it would take more hours to get back, but if they reached the herd close in, the current would push them back to the island. They would have less distance to go over the shore ice.

One time they started to go out at two o'clock in the morning. This was in May when the sun never sets. I had had only one or two hours of sleep. This was my first experience walrus hunting with the older persons and it was a good thing that I had a Thermos of coffee with me. The older men kept paddling hard and I tried to follow them. My uncle had taught me to paddle with my kayak but I was getting very tired. Finally they stopped, and one man climbed up on a **pressure ridge** of ice to look around. I reached for my coffee and got a little zip to moisten my mouth. It kept me going. They started off again in their kayaks and somehow I kept up with them, about fifteen older men.

We got about ten walrus that day. When I got home my mother was really glad because I could follow the older hunters. She said I was ready for anything.

Quagluk is holding bull-heads—bottom fish. We fished for bullheads through the ice with baleen fishing lines and Eskimo fishing hooks. The hooks had three parts: one stone (which could be a sparkle stone), a piece of lead, and a piece of walrus ivory with a copper or brass hook.

~4~

GOING OUT TO HUNT

When I was growing up on King Island, it did not seem to be hard work at all. I enjoyed life because that is the way I was brought up. In truth, it was really hard work, but magically I did not feel it. I went out hunting all day long, and I was really tired when I came in. After I slept, I was rested. I did not have feelings of tiredness. When I woke up I was ready to go out again whenever the weather was good.

I had to learn how to make many things and how to hunt and to survive out in the ice. On King Island we did not know what would happen in another three hours if we were walking out in the ice. If we did not have the right equipment, we would be lost; we would be dead.

We carried most of our equipment in a hunting bag. The hunting bag was made from an old sealskin that had been used as a float for a couple of years. To make a float, a new sealskin was sewn up and filled with air. It was used to help float dead oogruks and walrus back to the island. After a couple of years the skin didn't float anymore because its pores had been opened, but it was weatherized. Then we used it for a hunting bag. If the bag was not weatherized, it would get wet and be much heavier when the weather was bad, with rain and snow mixed.

The hunting bag was about three feet long and two feet wide. We carried it on our backs with a strap over our chests. If we fell in the water, we could pull it off fast. We did not have any buckles. It was the same with the rifle case; it had one strap with no buckles. We put the gun in the

Charles Mayac and John Alvanna hold seal poke floats and harpoons. The men are cross-cousins. Charles is my wife's oldest brother. John is both a cross-cousin and a partner-cousin to me.

James Ahrusak is wearing his full-winter hunting equipment. The wolverine ruff protects him from the freezing cold. He has his spear and his walking stick and a harpoon line around his neck. The white parka is for camouflage on the ice.

case and we just had to swing it around and pull the gun out. If we were walking alongside the open water and a seal suddenly came up, we had to get the gun in a hurry.

On the back of the hunting bag were two straps so we could tie snowshoes onto the bag. If we sat down on the ice next to the open water, we used the hunting bag as a cushion. We put the snowshoes under the hunting bag as protection, so it did not get wet.

To make snowshoes we had to find a young willow tree growing out in the **tundra**, or on a hillside. We cut one piece about two lengths of our arms, and that would be the right length for the frame of the snowshoes. We used hand measurements for making holes on the sides of the frame. Our snowshoes were small because the snow at King Island is more compact than the snow on the mainland. If you walk out by the trees on the mainland, the snow is soft. On the mainland they use bigger snowshoes. At King Island our snowshoes were mostly for walking on slush ice. For the rawhide bindings on the snowshoes, we used skins of spotted seal because these are much stronger than common sealskins. On the top part of the snowshoes we used common sealskin because it is much thinner.

Inside the hunting bag we carried a long piece of oogruk hide about two inches wide, and another line a half inch wide. We could attach these to a seal and drag it. We also had rope for emergency uses. If we killed a seal or a polar bear, we needed to bind them with lines, so we kept a good mixture of lines in our hunting bags.

We also had a raincoat in the hunting bag. It was a main item of survival gear. If I fell into the water my parka would get wet through in less than five minutes. It would freeze and stand away from my body and not keep in my body heat. If this happened, I would put the raincoat on under the parka and tie the string around my waist. The heat of my body would slowly dry the parka. The raincoat was made of bearded-seal intestine or walrus intestine.

We carried a bundle of hay in the bag to make extra insoles for our mukluks. If we fell in the water and the water got inside our mukluks, we had to change the insoles. We did not use felt insoles when we went out hunting because hay was lighter.

We always carried a piece of walrus intestine about one foot long. If we got thirsty, we filled the intestine with snow and put it under our parkas. Our body heat melted the snow. So we had water to drink. We did not eat snow. If you swallow snow, you get gas. If you do not have water, slush is good. You let the slush melt in your mouth and drink a little from it. You spit out the rest because it will make gas develop in your stomach.

I have been taught how to get water. If I were away from the island and walking on thin ice—there is no snow on new ice—I could make a little hole in the ice. The first water that came up I could drink because it is not too salty. Underneath the thin ice there is a little bit of fresh water between the ice and the salt water—not more than one mouthful.

We wore only one T-shirt and a parka when we went out hunting. With too many clothes we would get exhausted quickly when we dragged the seal. A fur parka was all we needed. Our body heat had to escape. We carried an extra shirt in our hunting bags for sleeping on the ice.

~5~

How We Hunted

I had to learn hunting methods from my uncles and my older brother. I learned to do things in a certain way from the older people. I learned about each animal, the way it could be approached and killed, and how it should be handled for use later.

Probably we Eskimos know more about the animals around King Island than anybody else. We know the sound the oogruk makes when it goes down into the water in springtime, in the month of March. It makes about four notes that sound like a musical instrument deep down in the ocean. I think the sounds are made either while eating or mating. We could hear the sounds about a mile away when we were out hunting in our kayaks. We used our paddles—we put them in the water and listened to them—to try to pinpoint where the sounds came from. Then we timed our paddling to the sounds. As the big bearded seals made the sounds, we stroked quickly, twice on one side, twice on the other side. When a seal is making the sounds, it cannot hear. If we used our paddles after the seal made the sounds, it would be disturbed easily.

Bubbles would float up to the surface of the water and the big bearded seal would come up near the bubbles. If we disturbed the animal, that would be the last time we would see it. We had to approach the seal very quietly. When the seal came up, we sat still. When we were near enough, we used a harpoon.

We did not always hunt the oogruk with our kayaks. Sometimes, in the wintertime, we went out on foot. Each hunter covered a different area.

TOP ➤ **T**hese four men went out hunting early in March. On the left is *Stanislau Muktoyuk, second is Joachim Koyuk, third is Phillip Tatayuna, and I am on the right. It was a good hunting day, and we each have a seal. We used our spears for killing animals, for testing the thickness of the ice, and for cutting through ice ridges. On our backs we carry rifles in bleached sealskin bags, and hunting bags made of seal. Our survival items are in the hunting bags, and our snowshoes are tied behind them.*

In the background are pressure ridges where the current has pushed the ice against the island. Most of the ice is underneath the surface, and sometimes it goes all the way to the bottom of the ocean.

BOTTOM ➤ **T**he men are *dragging a walrus skin. I weighed about six hundre pounds. They pulled it close to the island so the women could dress it for skin boat cover. At King Island we did not use do teams for hauling becaus the ice was too rough.*

If a hunter found a breathing hole in the ice, he signaled the other people in the area by making a big circle over his head with one arm. If he shouted, the seal would hear him. To show that it was a common-seal hole, the hunter patted his leg. If it were an oogruk hole, he would pat his head. We all knew those signals.

When somebody killed a big bearded seal on the ice, he made a loud sound to alert other hunters. When the hunters heard the signal, they would know an oogruk had been killed. All the hunters would run toward the person who had killed it. The seal would be divided among the hunters who ran in to help. The first person to reach the hunter got the breast meat; the second and third got the hindquarters; the fourth and fifth got the forequarters; the sixth got the spinal bones; the seventh got the neck bones; and the eighth got the skull. The hunter got the ribs and lower vertebrae.

A big bearded seal weighs about seven hundred pounds and it takes five men to pull one in. The meat was divided out on the ice. In our hunting bags we carried a small part of the walrus stomach to use as a container for meat. That way we did not get our hunting bags messed up. Some blood always drains out of the animal. The blood could be scraped up from the snow and put into the walrus stomach. When we got home we would boil the snow and make it into soup.

A *Native carving of a hunting scene, with the hunter ready to harpoon a polar bear*

"TAKE YOUR SEAL TO THAT OLDER PERSON"

When we killed any kind of animal for the first time, we had to give it to an older person. This was the Eskimo way. There is a story about a hunter a long time ago who got a seal. He did not want anybody to touch it. It was the only seal he managed to kill in his lifetime. From this story we learned that we had to give away our first animal, no matter how valuable it was. My first walrus, my first common seal, my first big bearded seal, my first polar bear—I had to give all of them away. A common seal and birds we gave to one person. It was the same with a big bearded seal. A walrus we shared out among a number of people.

My uncle picked who I should give an animal to. If an older person was hunting nearby, I had to take the animal to that person. When I got my first seal, we saw an older person nearby and my uncle told me, "Take your seal to that older person." If there was no hunter around, we took the animal to the village and my uncle named the older person I should give the skin and the meat to. We considered a person older when he did not go out hunting much anymore.

About one week after the hunt our relatives gave a dance for the animal we had killed. They said, "That animal you killed is going to vomit more birds and animals for you in later years." That is what the dancing was for, to make a young man a successful hunter.

We also learned about the cloud formations. My uncle taught me. In wintertime snow crystals fall when it starts to get cold. When we saw

This is the first part of the Wolf Dance. Five men and five women are dancing. The Wolf Dance has a very long story: it tells about a wolf presented by an eagle to a hunter. The mother of the wolf is upset because she has lost her son.

The dancers' gloves are sealskin with ivory rattles and polar-bear-fur trim. The headdresses are made of eagles' feathers. The gloves and headdresses were handed down through generations.

snow crystals coming down from the clouds, that meant it was going to be windy later. Also we could tell where there was open water when the weather was cloudy. Above the open water we could see a dark, sort of black, cloud.

When I was hunting one spring with my uncle, I made a big mistake. There is a special way to set a harpoon and harpoon line on top of a kayak. There are two bindings right on top of the kayak. A floating seal poke is attached to the kayak by a line. That line is pulled underneath the two bindings. When the hunter spears a seal, he pulls the animal in and throws the seal poke. What I did was put the line underneath the bindings so that I could not pull it out. I speared the seal and tried to pull it in. Instead it pulled me. I knew that I had done something wrong. The seal pulled on the line and broke it. I lost the seal and my harpoon!

When we got to the shore ice, I told my uncle about it. That was the day! He really gave me some hard words. He said I could have been pulled over in my kayak and drowned. My uncle did not want me to drown out there like my father. He wanted to teach me everything I needed to know to survive. He gave me some hard words for my survival. He did not say anything bad. He said, "You have to do it the right way." After that I looked twice before I attached my harpoon line to the seal poke.

John Alvanna is winding rawhide cut from the skin of a young oogruk, or big bearded seal, around a large wooden spool. The women would do the skin-sewing, but the men cut the rawhide strips.

~7~

MEDICINE MEN AND WOMEN WERE PROTECTORS

In the way of religion I would compare King Island beliefs with the religion of the Old Testament. We sacrificed some game in order to have more game in the future. The first time I killed a little bird my relatives skinned it. They saved the skin and hung it up. Then they had a dance to honor the bird. This was to encourage me to be a successful hunter; the dance said that the little bird would vomit more game for me in the future.

When we killed any kind of animal, we honored it. If a hunter killed a polar bear, he put a little bit of water inside its mouth so it could drink, so another bear could come back the next year. There was no big ceremony to honor the bear, just a little ceremony in order to get more animals for the village in the future.

Our **medicine men and women** danced for good weather and cured the sick, found some lost articles, and protected the village from unknown, powerful demons that came in during the dances at night. The medicine men and women were protectors. They could see a demon right away and make it go away. Otherwise the demon would destroy some of the villagers. When a demon appeared at the clubhouse in our village, where we were dancing, the medicine man immediately had the power. He went into a trance, then he beat the drum and scared away the demon.

The people used to say that if any kind of spirit wanted to come into a house, you would hear a big bang on top of the house. Then when the spirit started to enter, a fog would come in first and the seal-oil lamp

Phillip Tatayuna holds a walrus stomach, which will be cut up to make Eskimo drum heads. It is blown up to dry so that it will not wrinkle. Phillip was my cross-cousin. He used to work with my father. When I grew up and I wanted to build a skin boat, Phillip helped me. He went out hunting with me. He treated me as my father would have.

would flicker. There is a story about two young children who stayed at their house during the dances one night. There was a loud bang on top of their house and the children were scared because they had been told about demons. A fog filled the entranceway of their house, then a spirit came in. It was their dead grandfather, coming in as a human. But he came in backwards, not showing his face. He said, "There is a big, scary demon waiting to come into your house, so I came to protect you." The spirit in the form of their grandfather stayed all evening to protect the children. After the dances were over, the parents came home. They slipped on the stairs, maybe on the demon. The spirit flew up and away, right through the walls of the house. The children tried to follow the spirit of their grandfather, but they hit the wall instead of going through it and came back to their parents.

The medicine men and women had equal power. They travelled up in space, their souls travelled, their spirits travelled. This power existed in certain persons. If a person liked to have that power, he or she could accept it. If a person did not want to use the power, he or she could reject it. A medicine man or woman had to perform to demonstrate the power. There were stories about medicine men and women from different villages competing with each other. They swallowed things to demonstrate their powers. If a person was sick, the medicine man or woman needed a drum—an Eskimo drum—to perform. An intestine raincoat could do also, so that the medicine man or woman could be possessed by the spirit.

Robert Nuyakok was a kind of village doctor who set dislocated joints and massaged sore body areas. He was also an ivory carver. When we had contests of throwing stones or pebbles, he could hit any object.

All the villagers had to be in their houses because a medicine man or woman could not get the power if anyone was stepping on the snow or the ground outside. The medicine men and women performed mostly at night, when people were in their houses.

The medicine men and women knew when any hunter drifted away from the island. They knew because they heard a loud crack on the house of the hunter's relatives. If the crack came from the top of the relative's house, that meant the hunter was all right; everything was okay. But if the loud crack came from underneath the house, the hunter was dead.

In 1949 three men drifted out from King Island and only one came back. One of the men who was lost was my third cousin, Pahina. His grandparents heard a loud crack underneath their house and they knew that he was dead. Another man was named Ayac. In his house his extra pair of mukluks was hanging from a rafter in the ceiling. His mother watched them during the night when everyone was sleeping. If the mukluks swayed back and forth just a little bit, it meant the hunter was still alive. Father Cunningham, our priest, even came to the house and blessed the mukluks so that any demons would be chased away. And it happened that the mukluks were still moving. Ayac survived after being lost for seventeen days in the Chukchi Sea. Seventeen days!

We had a Catholic church on King Island beginning in the early 1920s. Father LaFortune came in the early 1920s and many people on King Island saw and heard him and accepted the Catholic Church. In 1938 Father Hubbard came to visit King Island and took pictures of us and the island. He put a "Christ the King" statue on the island and demons were never heard from again.

The *Northland*, a United States Coast Guard ship, brought the "Christ the King" statue in the spring. It is a bronze statue about five feet tall. Of course it was heavy. All the men on King Island lined up along a rope and they pulled it up. Every time the men on one side lifted the statue, the men above pulled it. It took almost a day to get it to the top of the

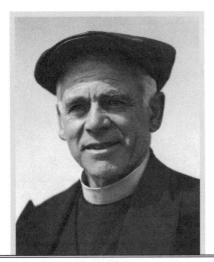

The "Christ the King" statue is made of bronze. It was placed at the top of the island and could be seen from the village, from the sea, and from the air.

Father LaFortune was our priest for fifteen years. He rarely left the island. If old folks stayed on the island in the summer, when the younger villagers went to the mainland, Father LaFortune stayed too.

mountain because it was so heavy and everybody got tired. The islanders were pleased about having the statue because ten years before an old person had dreamed about it. He dreamed that a shiny thing had come down from the sky and landed where the "Christ the King" statue was placed.

Before the statue was brought to the island, we had unusual activities, unexplained activities, that some people said were caused by a demon. Long ago, before I was born, maybe before Christianity existed, a woman fell on the east side of the island and died. She became a demon, a really strong demon. She had killed three of her brothers long before. If she wanted to tease a person, a hunter, she caused the land and the sea to vibrate. She hollered beneath the water and caused everything to vibrate. The hunter would see all kinds of game—walrus, bears, seals, whales, birds. And the mainland seemed to be only about a mile away, when it was really thirty-five miles away. The demon would appear at the top of the island and glide down into the water. A second later she would appear again at the top. In the wintertime she had a breathing hole in the ice, and if a hunter saw just one hair of her head through the breathing hole, she would holler and then attack him.

After a hunter had seen the demon he would return to the village, having forgotten everything that had happened, unless he started to bleed. Then a person could ask him, "What happened to you? You're bleeding," and the hunter would remember everything. You see, the demon had caused him to bleed because she was so powerful. (Also, maybe he was bleeding from exhaustion.)

After the "Christ the King" statue was placed on the island, the demon's activities completely stopped. We were not afraid anymore. Christianity brought security to us. Before that the medicine men and women were security for the village.

Some villagers on other islands and on the mainland reported seeing a glow over the island after the statue went up. People on Little Diomede Island and on Wales and Teller saw it sometimes in the 1940s. They thought the village might be burning. The glow is still seen at night sometimes, even now when there is nobody there. It is unexplainable, beyond my knowledge.

An older person on King Island once told me about a medicine man who said that this universe has a creator. He said that if you eat the flesh and drink the blood of this universe's creator, you will be safe. This was before anyone on King Island had heard anything about Christianity.

A Stepfather, Uncles, and Cousins

When I was a child on King Island I was poor because my father had died. But as I grew up, I started to get some things. I learned to hunt; I had good hunting equipment made for me by my uncles. I was physically fit. I started to feel that I could take anything; I could do anything. I had been trained to take care of myself and I got a lot of exercise.

Then my mother remarried. I liked my stepfather but he had a mother-in-law who I hated. You see, his first wife had died, but his first wife's mother still visited him. She would come into our house, nagging at my mother, even though my mother did not do anything wrong. I had really bad feelings about this woman because she upset my mother. Sometimes my mother cried.

My stepfather did not stop her because she was his in-law. We could not say anything to in-laws. It was not allowed in the Eskimo way. No matter what our in-laws did, we could not say anything.

Finally that woman died, but I did not forget her. When I was about nineteen I said something mean about her in the clubhouse, in front of my uncle. I said, "I wish that woman were alive right now. When she came into the clubhouse, I would throw her out into the cold." My uncle was related to her also. He was her brother-in-law, so he gave me a really bad eye. He told my cousin to talk to me. My cousin told me (it came from my uncle, really) that when a poor person starts to get something, he becomes hard to other people. My uncle believed that I was starting to do

This is my wife, Clara, when she was about eighteen. She is coming back from the underground shelter where we stored meat.

Our parents picked our wives, our husbands. If the parents thought a young man could support a family, they would allow the marriage. That is how we got married. I was dating my wife before my mother chose her. I would invite her to a dance. We went for walks. We did not like to show ourselves in public because if our cross-cousins saw us they would tease us the next day.

something bad because I had been poor and I was beginning to have something. He told my cousin to tell me a story so that I would understand that I was starting to make problems within myself and for the village. I understood right away and stopped.

Our behavior was ruled by relationships. When a person was bad, when a person started to make problems for another person, relationships came in. The first time maybe a cousin or an uncle would tell the person not to do it. They always gave a person another chance.

Cross-cousins are very important in our culture. When a husband and a wife have a son and a daughter, the son's children are cross-cousins with the daughter's children. If the family had two boys and one girl, the two boys' children were partner-cousins. They were cross-cousins to the one girl's children. Same way if there were two daughters and one son. The two girls' children were partner-cousins and they were cross-cousins to the one boy's children.

It is very confusing. My mother and my aunt told me at a young age who were my partner-cousins and who were my cross-cousins. I do not really know the history of how the system came about, but it united our village government. That is how our village government controlled, with cross-cousins and partner-cousins. Cross-cousins were supposed to tease each other, to make fun of each other when somebody did something wrong. Partner-cousins were supposed to help each other throughout life.

Cross-cousins could make any kind of jokes and try to make each other feel bad. And if a person lost his or her temper because of something a cross-cousin said, he or she would be called a bad apple. Whenever someone misbehaved or did something foolish, someone would tell that person's cross-cousin about it and the cross-cousin would tease, make up jokes or songs, to make the person feel funny. This went on throughout life.

Partner-cousins would stick together, talk to each other, and work

My *Aunt Nereruk is babysitting for her daughter, packing her grandson.
She was a really strong woman. She could pack a two-hundred-pound
walrus skin, even when she was carrying a baby.*

My first cousin, Ellanna, is with her daughter, Cecilia. Ellanna used to make mukluks for me. When I grew up, I gave her whole seals to return the service.

together. If a person got in trouble, a partner-cousin would feel bad about it. If one partner-cousin thought the other one was causing a problem for someone, the cousin would not say anything directly. A person would not call a partner-cousin a problem to his or her face but would tell a cross-cousin about it and the cross-cousin would do all he or she could to make the problem person feel funny.

People observed and knew whether someone was bad or not. Often they gave a person a second chance, a third chance. They tried to make a relationship with a problem person. They did not just ignore the person because then he or she would become more of a problem.

Sometimes things happened. A person had a big mouth and made things hard for another person, over and over. Finally the troublemaker might be killed. Sometimes the uncle of the murdered person, or some other relative, would decide to take revenge, maybe kill the murderer. He would do this to satisfy himself, but this upset the village more.

Mostly we used our dancing to get rid of our frustration and anger. If we did not have anything to do because the weather was bad, we got frustrated. Dancing, singing, and laughing with each other cured our feelings. If a person lost his wife and was depressed and did not want to be helped, a cousin or grandfather would say, "You should go over and join the dances. You are going, going down, trying to bring back the memory of your wife. Go over and join the dances." So he would do that and he would forget the bad things, and a couple of weeks later he would be better. His mind could think of something besides the loss.

This is my mother-in-law. She and my father-in-law were nice to me. I did what they wanted me to do, and in return, they gave me anything I asked for. When I was first married, my wife and I went to Nome. My father-in-law said, "When you go to Nome, do not go with bad people." That meant not to go in the bars. In Eskimo culture we cannot refuse anything that has been said by our in-laws, so I did not drink for twenty years. I was a heavy drinker before I married. I started drinking just before I went into the service in World War II. Good thing I stopped drinking because otherwise my kids might have worn torn clothes and had nothing to eat.

My mother-in-law provided for us—clothing, instruction, and babysitting. And my in-laws provided a lot of help to my wife and my mother.

WORLD WAR II

People on King Island did not always know what was happening in the world. We did not have much political knowledge and could not understand other places.

We had radios at King Island and the teachers had a two-way radio. Whenever we wanted to report some news from King Island, we called Nome on the two-way radio; and when people in Nome had news, they called King Island. Sometimes we sent telegrams to our relatives to ask them how they were, and they answered. But most of our news we got by two-way radio. We had a schedule for calling in the morning and in the afternoon. If the reception was bad in the morning, we called in the afternoon.

During the Second World War, there were two men on King Island who understood a little English. They wrote down the news from the radio broadcasts and gave the information to our priest, Father LaFortune. He was a white priest, French Canadian, but he spoke English and he spoke Eskimo as we did. He was with the King Island people for fifteen years or more. He lived in a little house by himself. He ate just like us and spoke like us. He gave half the sermon in Eskimo.

Father LaFortune told us what was happening in the Second World War. We did not understand what was wrong, why countries were fighting each other. What was the cause? What was the reason that they were fighting? We did not have the knowledge to understand these problems. A lot of times people would say, "What the heck are they doing, fighting each other, killing people? They cannot eat human beings. They should come here to Alaska and hunt some animals for their food." That was what the older folks at King Island said. "How come they kill each other? They cannot eat the bodies of the human beings they kill."

I was drafted into the United States Army during the Second World War. Quite a few men from the village passed the physical examination. But the ones who really did not understand English were not drafted, and those who were too old or had medical problems were not drafted. I spoke a little English so I was taken. I was sent to Nome for basic training. Some men were sent out of Alaska, over toward Japan, but most of us were stationed in Alaska. One of the King Island boys was stationed in Dutch Harbor in the Aleutian Islands when the Japanese bombed the town. He said he was really scared because he could hear the bombs whistling down.

One summer the people on King Island saw Japanese artillery in the area. One man was walking on top of the island and he saw a boat coming in. He went to warn the villagers. They waited and waited and waited but nothing happened. The boat was a submarine that submerged before getting to the land. The villagers never saw it again.

It is very hard to land a boat at King Island. There is no sandbar to land on; there are only boulders. Even though we had lived at King Island throughout our lifetimes, we had to search for the right place to land sometimes. We had to land in seconds, before the breakers came in. If we did not pull the boat out of the water right away, the waves would break the boat. Anyone who did not know how to land would lose the boat. So it was not likely that King Island could be attacked by sea.

A bush pilot [a pilot who flies small planes in remote areas] once landed a plane on the island. He landed on top of the island, heading uphill. Taking off, he just slid down the hill. He was a really good pilot, I would say. The only place for a plane to land most of the time was on the

Ahnatook is holding a baby seal brought in by her father, John Ollanna. The seal pup was born early in April. Her father brought it home so she could play with it for a while. Then it was killed and the fur was used for trimming moccasins and parkas.

shore ice. Sometimes we made a temporary landing strip down there. We moved rocks and snow to make a flat runway. There were a few bush pilots who knew how to land on the shore ice.

We were ready for any kind of action at King Island. We had our army rifles, we were trained. Everyone knew how to shoot at King Island anyway. We knew the island just like the palms of our hands. If an enemy had ever tried to get onto King Island we knew what to do, where to hide, how to sleep on the ice. We would have had no problems.

~10~

I PROVE MYSELF A HUNTER

I had been in the army for only one month, training in Nome, when there was an accident and I broke my leg. I was helping to unload a transport ship, moving some lumber. The sling slipped out from under some timbers and the lumber fell on me. I was put into the hospital in Nome but the doctors did not set the fracture properly and infection set in. That month the Japanese invasion started in the Aleutian Islands and the doctors were trying to make room in the hospital for wounded soldiers. So they transferred quite a few patients, including me, to Barnes General Hospital in Vancouver, Washington. By this time gangrene had set into my leg. The doctors at Barnes said that if I had been sent sooner, they could have tried to save my leg, but it was too late. So they had to do three operations to amputate my leg. It was very painful.

I was sent to Bushnell General Hospital in Brigham City, Utah, to be fitted with a wooden leg. I was there about five months. I felt that I wanted to die. All my preparation to be a good hunter was lost. I had lost everything. I could not go out hunting on the moving ice any more. The Bering Sea ice moves all the time—north, south, east, and west—and it is very dangerous. It is a very dangerous place to be even with two legs.

After I was discharged from the army and sent back home, my cousin made me crutches. I was disappointed, angry, and depressed. The people who had a close relationship to me said that they had lost somebody who would have been a successful hunter. They had tried to prepare me especially to be a polar bear hunter. That is partly what all the running had been for, to build my muscles to run after polar bears. And I had lost that. I was twenty-one years old and I had lost everything.

I decided that I would hunt anyway. What else could I do? I made heavier crutches so that I could walk on the ice. Starting out, I tried to hunt mostly on the shore ice, because that ice does not move. I carried my rifle and my hunting bag over my shoulders and I moved across the shore ice using my crutches.

One day the weather was nice, the current was not fast, and the wind was calm. When the wind is calm, the current is slow. I went out hunting and I got myself a seal. I felt pretty good about it. I had gone out onto the moving ice and I had been successful hunting. I started to drag the seal toward the shore ice. I took a line from my hunting bag, tied it around the seal and around my waist, and headed home. I did not get very far. A lead opened up in front of me, open water, and I fell in, inside the moving ice. I could not get out. Good thing there was somebody nearby. I hollered at him and he came running and pulled me out.

Another time I went out hunting on the moving ice and I lost my rifle. I was catching a seal and I had some of my equipment out near its breathing hole. My hunting bag and my rifle were some distance away. The ice cracked between me and my rifle and I could not jump over the split. I could not get my rifle. The lead was only about two or three feet wide. Anybody else could have jumped it but I could not. So I made a really long walk around the lead to try to get my hunting bag, but the ice cracked again and the rifle sank. The hunting bag was floating in the water but I could not get it. It would have been saved if I had two legs. So I said to myself finally, "If I try to go out hunting on crutches, one day I will not come back. It is too dangerous."

So I built myself a little skin boat, about sixteen feet long. My brother's son and my brother helped me make the wooden frame. Some of the women of the village sewed the split walrus hides to cover the frame. I

The women of the village are making a cover for a skin boat from split walrus hide. The outside layer of hide is used for the cover. Three or four skins are sewn together with waterproof stitches. We use the inside layer of the hide for the inside of the skin-boat frame so that our belongings will not get wet.

thought I could hunt from a skin boat more safely than on crutches. Whenever the north wind blew, I hunted in the open water on the south side of the village. That way I started getting more seals. I had used a kayak to hunt seals before my accident, but I could not balance myself anymore in a kayak with my wooden leg. To balance my kayak I had to lean toward one side and it was very hard on my back. So I never used the kayak anymore. I used the little skin boat.

The people at King Island tried to be helpful to me. One winter my nephew, my brother, and I went out hunting on the east side of the island.

We went out until we could not go out any farther because the area was closed in with ice and the skin boat could not go through. We pulled our little skin boat on top of the ice. I looked north and saw some object above the pressure ridge of ice off in the distance. And above the object were two ravens flying.

Now when I was young, my mother used to tell me that whenever my father saw two ravens playing with something on the ice, that meant that an animal was there, maybe a fox or maybe a polar bear! I saw those two ravens go down and go up and go down and go up. I kept looking where they went down in the distance and I saw that object, and I knew it was a polar bear. I told my brother and my nephew, "There is a polar bear coming toward us. Maybe we should pull our skin boat up some more so that it will not be carried away by the ice." So we pulled it up a little way from the water.

We went behind the big pressure ridges and we hid. We saw that there were three polar bears, a mother and two cubs almost the same size as the mother. Every time we looked, they had come closer. They could not see us, only our skin boat. They may have thought the boat was a seal or a walrus. Finally, as they started to move away from us, we each took aim at one polar bear and we shot all three.

My mother was still alive then and when we came home she asked me, "Did you kill that polar bear, son?" I said, "Yes," and she began crying for joy. She had thought I would not be able to kill a polar bear with my wooden leg, but I managed to get one. We used the meat for food and we sold the fur.

We had a polar bear dance about a week later. We gave away some food, rawhide, and furs from the animals. I was manager of the co-op store in the village then and I ordered an ice-cream maker that year, to make ice cream the white people's way. That was the first time we served ice cream at a polar bear dance. And the next day one of my close relatives said, "Paul, you should get another polar bear so that we can have more ice cream."

This is a party for a polar bear hunter. Leo Kunnuk is giving away **agutaq,** or Eskimo ice cream. The old man on the right, Matthew Anasungok, is making up a new polar bear song. He puts in words about where the man hunted the polar bear, whether the man killed the bear on new ice or young ice, and about the polar bear's actions.

I think I hunted every type of animal at King Island—seals, walrus, polar bears, birds. I did what I had prepared for before I became handicapped. My preparation to be a good hunter was not wasted. When I started to hunt from my little skin boat, I could keep up with the other hunters. I never tried to be a great hunter but only to keep up with the others. But I proved myself to be a hunter—not a handicapped person, but a hunter.

~11~
LOOKING BACK

My wife and I lived on King Island until 1956 when we moved to Nome. We lived in Nome for twelve years. I did some ivory carving, some janitorial work to support my family. And I was still hunting. The people on King Island started moving to Nome in 1948 to get jobs and because of medical problems. We moved to Nome because of health problems also. The major health problem on the island was tuberculosis. Our people picked it up from whalers and from people in Nome. It was a deadly disease for Alaskans. A lot of us went to Nome because family members were hospitalized at the Native sanatorium at Mount Edgecombe in Southeast Alaska, or at Orangeside in Seattle. We wanted to be closer to them.

No one had travelled much before that time, then tourism came in and offered us a chance to travel. We were good dancers on King Island and the airlines offered to take us stateside, to promote their business. They took Native dancers to Seattle, Los Angeles, San Francisco, New York, and Washington, D.C. The airlines encouraged us to dance for tourists in Nome and Anchorage.

After some people had left King Island, the government forced the rest out. The **Bureau of Indian Affairs** is the government agency that is supposed to be responsible for Native Americans. The BIA condemned the island school and did not replace it. The families with kids had to move to Nome to get them some sort of education, a different education from the Native way. The last family moved from King Island in 1969.

Paul, *with* Bear of the North, *a model schooner that he carved. The hull is made of baleen, with ivory dowels. The railings are of walrus ivory, the mast of walrus jawbone, and the rolled sails of walrus intestine.*

A *traditional Inupiat game was making string pictures. Paul shows how to make a string dog sled at the Smithsonian Institution.*

Since then no family has moved back because there is no teacher. The only people who go back are single people or some whose children are grown up.

One reason the Bureau of Indian Affairs gave for moving us away from King Island was danger from the rocks. The BIA told the King Islanders, "There's a big rock above the village. Experts say it is going to come down any time and the school and some of the houses are in its path." The rock is still up there. It never rolled down. The BIA made excuses for locking the island. I do not know what the government is trying to do for Native people. A lot of times I just reject the idea of the BIA.

In 1967 I came to Anchorage for a meeting of Alaska Legal Services to represent the northwest part of the state. I was hired by the Alaska Centennial people to work in tourism. My wife and I decided we could make a living here. We go back to Nome and King Island in the summer.

After the Centennial [a celebration of the hundredth anniversary of the purchase of Alaska from Russia in 1867], I worked for the Alaska Native Welcome Center and then the State of Alaska as an employment interviewer. After that, on the Trans-Alaska Pipeline, I was a site counselor at a pump station. I worked with the superintendent, supervisors, and foremen on Native hire as a middleman to help communication between the supervisors and the Native workers. I worked for nearly a year at the Seward Skill Center as a recreation director. Then for ten years I was employed at the Cook Inlet Native Association as a cultural coordinator. I worked with our Native people as they adjusted to urban life.

The influence of modern society is very confusing for our Native people. We are told that we have to go to school to make a living, more income, cash for our pockets to buy better things. In order to be somebody, we are encouraged to finish grade school, finish high school, finish college.

But when we go to school, we lose our own culture. Concerned persons say we should retain our culture, but to do that we have to go back into the old ways. The only income we get from living by Native culture is food for our families. In the Native way, everything was given by nature. We have to learn to compete with Mother Nature, and nobody knows what Mother Nature is going to do. Even in California there are droughts and nothing grows. Even modern society cannot beat Nature. To live the Native way, we must have instruction or we will be lost. We will be dead.

If I really wanted to go back to King Island, I would go back. But my family says no. The family has to make decisions also. The man does not have to make decisions all the time. If my family members think they can make a better living here in Anchorage, I go along with them even though I want to go back to Nome, closer to King Island. If I took my family to King Island, I would have to reteach them how to live by Mother Nature. But my kids do not want to go back because there is no income, there is no money involved if they go back to Native culture. My two girls went to the University of Alaska. They have good jobs here in Anchorage, and they cannot use the Native ways that I want to teach them.

I have tried to integrate myself into the working system of modern society. I am a school dropout, and I do not know much about writing or

Qawaliak is making a **cribbage board** out of walrus ivory. When he was a boy, his mother took him to a running stream in the fall of the year and put his hands in the cold water for a few minutes to make them tough. It worked. He could cut seals in the winter without mittens. He also composed Eskimo songs for the village.

about business. But I have been taught the Native ways since I was a kid, and I can earn an income by teaching about them. A lot of young people are trapped in the middle. They are dropouts and cannot find work because they do not have any experience. I am a little bit luckier because I have knowledge enough to do something with Native culture—like dancing, carving, telling stories, and explaining about Native ways.

The Bureau of Indian Affairs should give young people the whole picture of modern society. If a young person wants to be a plumber, for example, the BIA should send that person to trade school. But Native families are tight knit, and parents do not want their children to go away to learn a trade. A lot of families feel this way. I feel that way and my mother felt that way. I encourage my kids to go further in their schooling because it is the only way they can make a good living. There is a lot of competition when people seek jobs; this society will only accept somebody who has education enough to do some kind of work.

The biggest mistake of the federal government is the welfare system. We did not have a welfare system in my early days, but somehow we got through the winters. If you want to make a living, you have to go out and work at something. Welfare is a bad influence, a handout from the government, and it takes away pride from the Native tribes.

The United States government should talk to our elders and see what is the best way to teach or direct the King Island people. The only things the public schools teach now are the ABC's and arithmetic. They do not help with the problems that Native people meet during our lifetimes. When we try to integrate ourselves into the urban center, the shock is so great and the ways so hard to understand—the business part of the urban life—that we cannot go anywhere. Our kids have been changed so much in the modern system that they do not listen to the elders. The kids do not accept anymore.

The federal government should work with parents by explaining how the modern system works. When the government first came into the villages, Native people had no lawyers, state troopers, police officers, or correctional centers. The government started to influence us, telling us we required these agencies that were not required before because we had our own system. I did not see child abuse in our village when I was young. We did not have alcohol or drug problems. We did not have divorces.

We could make the two systems work together if the government sat down with us and made plans to educate our children both the modern way and the village way, to satisfy both sides. The teachers must sit down with us, and the lawyers, and the state troopers, and the police officers, and all the other government officials. We can teach these officials the Eskimo ways because they are the best ways for our people. And we can make a contribution to modern American society.

NOTE — *Paul Tiulana continued to contribute to the welfare of his people and his country. In 1983 he was named "Man of the Year" by the Alaska Federation of Natives, a statewide organization representing all the Alaska Native regions and cultures. In 1984 he was given a National Heritage Fellowship Award by the National Endowment for the Arts and he received a letter from President Ronald Reagan. The American Festival of Arts sent Paul and his wife, Clara, to London, England, in 1985 to demonstrate ethnic arts at the Museum of Mankind.*

Paul Tiulana died in 1994 at age seventy-three. Upon his death, the photo of him as a hunter (page 2) appeared on the front page of the Anchorage Daily News. *The funeral service drew many people of all races and religions. King Islanders sat in the front pews and sang a liturgy in their own language. The Roman Catholic Archbishop of Anchorage, Francis T. Hurley, described his visit to Paul at the hospital before he died. He gave Paul a blessing, and then Paul reached out his hands and blessed him. The archbishop said that he was surprised—such a thing had never happened before—but he appreciated a blessing from Paul Tiulana.*

THE PHOTOGRAPHER

Father Bernard R. Hubbard, S.J. dedicated a major
part of his long life to study, exploration, and religious service in Alaska.
His photographs of the King Island people form an especially beautiful part
of his work.

Bernard Rosencrans Hubbard was born in San Francisco in 1888.
His father, a college professor, owned land in the Big Basin Redwood area
south of San Francisco. Bernard explored the woods and mountains of
California at a time when travel to the countryside involved wild rides on
a stagecoach pulled by six horses.

At twenty, Bernard Hubbard entered the Jesuit order at Los Gatos,
California. Five years later he was teaching Latin, English, mathematics,
and history in a Jesuit college in Los Angeles. He also coached baseball
and football. Next, the order sent him to Mount St. Michael's House of
Philosophy in Spokane, Washington. He studied lava beds outside Spokane
and accompanied another priest, a scientist, on expeditions through the
Columbia River basin in eastern Washington, areas of Idaho and Mon-
tana, Glacier Park, and the Yellowstone region in Wyoming.

Father Hubbard made many trips to Europe. He studied theology in
Innsbruck, Austria, and spent holidays and summer vacations exploring
alpine peaks and glaciers. His guides named him "Gletscher Pfarrer"
which translates to Glacier Priest, a title he carried all his life.

He made his first trip to Alaska in 1927 to explore the Mendenhall and
Taku Glaciers. He took Santa Clara University students with him on later
trips. These expedition made Father Hubbard an expert on Alaska—its
glaciers, volcanoes, weather conditions, and some of its people. The team
took still and motion pictures, which Father Hubbard showed to hundreds
of thousands of people in nationwide lecture tours. He wrote many articles and two books, *Mush, You Malemutes* (1932) and *Cradle of the Storms*

(1935). Father Hubbard always carried his Mass kit, either in his back-pack or with his supplies on dog sleds. He stated, "Daily Mass and breviary meant everything to me . . . and in all my travelling, the schedules had to be made out so that neither the privilege nor the obligation would be endangered."

Between 1937 and 1939 Father Hubbard lived on King Island. He continued his glacier research and captured the King Island people on film. He supervised the erection of the statue "Christ the King." It served as an invitation to peace between the two hemispheres. King Island carvers presented Father Hubbard with two ivory carvings of the statue, which he took, with Eskimo greetings, to Pope Pius XII.

Father Hubbard's home base was Santa Clara University. He lived in Santa Clara during the latter part of his life, and there he deposited his vast collections of data, photographs, and motion pictures. He was planning another trip to Alaska when he died in 1962.

This biographical sketch of Father Hubbard is based upon material provided by Santa Clara University.

WRITING THE STORIES OF OUR ELDERS

If you would like to write a story as told by an elder, you can do it. You will create some living history and a work of art. It's not easy to do, but it's interesting and fun.

You need to find an elder who is willing to talk and who has at least one photograph from long ago. Or find one or more photographs from the past first, and then look for an elder who can tell you what's in the pictures.

Explain to the elder what you want to do, and ask permission to tape-record the elder's story or explanations. Many people will say no at first, but they will be secretly delighted. Once you ask for an elder's memories, you have an obligation to listen for a while. Memories are precious.

After you have made a tape, you will need to transcribe it by listening to the tape over and over and typing the words out on a computer or typewriter.

The next step is to pick out the story. Some people are natural storytellers; others are not. As the writer, you decide what to keep in and what to leave out. The story could be a description of a person, place, or event. You could use only a small part of the transcription—the section that, in your opinion, is the best part.

Tell the elder's story in his or her own words, but leave out clutter. Don't include the "uhhs" and "ahhs." Correct the grammar if necessary. You can change, "I didn't do nothing about it" to "I didn't do anything about it." Poor English does not read well, and it could embarrass the elder.

Now you are almost finished. Take the story and the photographs back to the elder for approval. Make sure that you got everything right. Ask the elder if you may send the story to a local paper or magazine for publication.

At this point some people think about money. They imagine royalties, riches, and fame. This is pure fantasy, as 99.9 percent of writers and their subjects are not rich. If you ask for payment at all, you will be lucky to get fifty dollars for your story and photographs. You don't do this for money. (If you do get any money, you should share it with the elder. It was a joint effort.)

Your living history may be published in a school paper, a church or temple newsletter, the local weekly advertiser, a magazine or a bigger daily newspaper. Wherever it ends up, it's recorded for others to enjoy.

Good luck!

GLOSSARY

Agutaq ～ A tangy-tasting dessert (called Eskimo ice cream by non-Natives) made of whipped reindeer fat and seal oil. It can be mixed with mossberries, salmon berries, or salmon.

Baleen ～ The black, horny, elastic material that hangs in fringed, parallel, platelike sheets from the upper jaw or palate of whalebone whales. Baleen serves as a strainer as the whales feed on tiny sea creatures.

Blubber ～ The fat of a sea mammal. The blubber is eaten with dry fish, seal, birds, and other foods. Oil rendered from the blubber is used as a dip or mixed in other foods. The oil is also used to coat leaves picked from the tundra and stored for later use.

Bureau of Indian Affairs (BIA) ～ An agency of the United States government that was established to deal legally with Native Americans.

Cribbage ～ A card game. Scores are kept with ivory pegs and a cribbage board.

Cross-cousins, partner-cousins ～ Cousins are classified either as cross- or partner-cousins as well as first, second, or third cousins. Imagine that your parents have two sons and one daughter. Offspring of these children are first cousins. The boys' children are partner-cousins to each other and the daughter's are cross-cousins to the boys'. Cross-cousins have the right to tease each other without giving offense. Partner-cousins are each other's confidants.

Driftwood ～ Wood drifting in the ocean or washed ashore from forested areas. The Arctic region is a treeless tundra where there is no wood.

Eskimo ～ A broad term used to describe a member of a group of Native North American people scattered through the area from Greenland across northern Canada and Alaska and into Siberia and the Russian Far East.

Harpoon ～ A long, rounded, wooden pole with a detachable spear. The pole is attached to a line and used to retrieve large sea mammals.

Igloo ～ A temporary shelter made of snow and used during snowstorms.

Inuit ～ Native people of Canada.

Inupiat ～ Native people of northern Alaska. The Inupiat language is similar from village to village, but each village has its own dialect. Other Alaskan Native groups include Central Yupik, Siberian Yupik, Aluutiq, Aleut, Tsimshian, Haida, Tlingit, and Athabaskan.

Kayak ⁓ An Eskimo canoe made of skins of bearded seals (oogruks) stretched over a frame of wood, with a center opening for a paddler.

Lead ⁓ An open channel of water in a field of ice.

Medicine men and women ⁓ People who guide others through life with special spiritual powers. These powers may be accepted or rejected by those who have them, and they are usually passed on from one generation to the next.

Moving ice ⁓ Ocean currents beneath the ice keep it moving. Arctic hunters have to be ever mindful of this movement, as it could sweep them away from the land.

Mukluks ⁓ Boots worn by Eskimos. The soles are made from skins of bearded seals that Native women crimp with their teeth. The upper parts are made from skins of seals or calves, or skins of reindeer or caribou legs.

Murre ⁓ Several swimming and diving birds that migrate to the Arctic region in the summer.

Parka ⁓ A pullover garment made of fur. The lining is made from skins with the hair turned toward the body. The covering is cloth trimmed with bias tape. The hood, sleeves, and hem of the parka are fur-trimmed to keep out the wind.

Pressure ridge ⁓ A raised line or strip on floating ice, produced by buckling or crushing caused by the force of winds or tides.

Seal poke ⁓ The skin of a seal that is left whole and used to store food, to keep hunting equipment dry, and to store clothing, like a duffel bag. The body of the seal and its fat are drawn out through the head. The special knives (ulus) used for this task leave the skin whole, except for the paws, which are sewn shut.

Skin boat ⁓ A boat made of walrus or other animal skin stretched over a wooden frame.

Snowbirds ⁓ Sparrowlike birds of North and Central America. They have gray or black heads and white outer tail feathers.

Tundra ⁓ The vast, nearly level, treeless plains of the Arctic regions.

Ulu—A knife with a rounded blade and a handle on top. Used by Eskimo women.

FOR MORE INFORMATION

For Older Readers

Andrews, Susan B., and John Creed. *Authentic Alaska: Voices of Its Native Writers.* Lincoln: Univers Nebraska Press, 1998.

Chaussonnet, Valerie. *Crossroads Alaska: Native Cultures of Alaska and Siberia.* Washington, D.C.: S sonian Institution, 1995.

Lowry, Shannon. *Natives of the Far North: Alaska's Vanishing Culture in the Eyes of Edward Sheriff C* Mechanicsburg, PA: Stackpole Books, 1994.

Oliver, Ethel Ross. *Favorite Eskimo Tales Retold.* Anchorage: Alaska Pacific University Press, 1992

For Middle Grade Readers

Murphy, Claire Rudolf. *Friendship Across Arctic Waters: Alaskan Cub Scouts Visit Their Soviet Neighbors.* New York: Lodestar Books, 1991.

Murphy, Claire Rudolf. *Native Cultures in Alaska.* Anchorage: Alaska Geographic, 1996.

Murphy, Claire Rudolf. *Sharing Alaska Native Cultures: A Hands-On Activity Book.* Fairbanks: University of Alaska Museum, 1993.

For Younger Readers

Hoyt-Goldsmith, Diane. *Arctic Hunter.* New York: Holiday House, 1992.

Miller, Debbie S. *A Polar Bear Journey.* Boston: Little, Northwest Books, 1997.

Murphy, Claire Rudolf. *A Child's Alaska.* Anchorage: Alaska Northwest Books, 1994.

Rogers, Jean. *King Island Christmas.* New York: Greenwilow Books, 1985.

INDEX